THE SAVVY CHILD WITHIN YOU

BECOME MORE SUCCESSFUL IN YOUR LIFE AND BUSINESS USING FORGOTTEN CHILDHOOD WISDOM

MEL CLIFFORD

REMEMBER TO PLAY LIKE CHILDREN, BY KEEPING THE SIMPLICITY, FUN, CLARITY AND HONESTY IN ALL THAT YOU DO IN YOUR LIFE AND BUSINESS WORLD

Author	Mel Clifford
Contact details	mel@melclifford.com
Cover Design	Trent Janisch
Published by	Seanchaí Press
	info@seanchaipress.com
	www.seanchaipress.com
Drawings & Sketches	Many thanks to the individuals who share their free photos on www.pixabay.com

ISBN No 978-0-9940351-6-5

Dedication

To Audrey, thank you for your love, friendship and for all your valuable discussions and encouragement to write.

To Paul, Jane, Ríain, Shannon Ben and Kym, thank you for your support and the learning you give me in my life. I know I have more to learn, I send you my unconditional love.

Learning helps you become your authentic self.

Rekindle that savvy child within you.

Acknowledgement

Thank you for opening these pages, my wish is that they will give you food for thought and add value into your life.

To all who have shared their words of encouragement, granting me the courage to follow my dreams and believe in myself. Everyone I've worked and shared my experience of business with, it was with you I learned my trade.

To Trent Janisch, for this book's cover design and your encouragement and support in providing valuable input into the structure of my work for this book.

To Connie Johnson, for her keen eye and great suggestions in reviewing this book.

To you the reader, I hope you enjoy the journey of this book.

Only when our writings are read does it give life to our words, please share these words with others as the more they are read the more life they gain.

No book should be left on a shelf to gather dust.

About the Author

 I began my career in my early teens, working at several part-time jobs during my school years. It was lots of fun. I learnt early on, that building relationships and having the ability to get on with people was vital to any success in business and life in general.

I learnt that people are far more important as human beings than the positions they hold. I believe that it's the person, not the position that makes the real difference in business. Because of this insight I have developed a passion for helping people to make the important changes they need to grow and to become the person they are meant to be. It is wonderful seeing people break free from old limitations towards happiness, knowing that I may have helped in some small way.

As I rose through the ranks to Director level within the retail sector, it became apparent to me that nurturing and maintaining honesty and curiosity (which comes so natural to a child) was absolutely essential for healthy growth in any area.

I know that integrity is vital in all our dealings with people and it is only I who can destroy it within me. Mind your character for it speaks plenty about who you are.

I have lead and developed my own business in people and project management where I travelled extensively for work in Europe, North America and China. From these wonderful years of experience, I have learned so much about what it takes for an organisation to thrive. My desire now, is to share with you, the reader, some of what I have learned. To help you make the most of your greatest commodity, your time; and empower you to take personal responsibility for your own growth and direction of your life. To let that child within you out into your business and personal worlds.

Wishing you only happiness, health and a positive influence in your journey in this world.

Enjoy the read **Mel**

"The things we fear most in organizations -- fluctuations, disturbances, imbalances -- are the primary sources of creativity."

Dr. Margaret J Wheatley

Contents

Make someone smile today

"I keep thinking, we teach children to use language to solve their disputes. We teach them not to hit and fight and bite. Then look what adults do!" - Naomi Shihab Nye

Some Thoughts

Why is it that when we enter the world of business (be that organisations for profit or not for profit) we seem to lose vital elements of our personalities? We are expected to behave in certain ways to align with "professionalism". We move into moods of authority, conflict, bullying, and greed. We come across with dishonesty, betrayal, lack of respect for others and low personal value. We enter the world of political games, egos and false measurements of success. Is this what business professionalism is? I believe we should choose to have integrity versus professionalism. What we have witnessed in many corporations is that being professional seems to equate to acting dishonestly.

Is it that we act this way and call it competition, or survival in the world of business? Phrases are used like: *"if you can't stand the heat get out of the kitchen"*, *"measure up to the plate"*, *"business is business"* or, *"it's just business"*, *"don't take it personally"*. The latest one is: *"Either get with the program or go"* direct from within the White House of the United States. All statements made to protect those that wish to use them for their own personal gain.

What about plain and simple, the value of truth, integrity and the respect for others in our world of business? Above all, being who you really are works best in one's life. I value my time. I call it as I see it. It might not be how others see it, but at least I am honest with myself and my own personal values. I value true respect for others and diversity in our world. I believe we need constant reminding of the simple things in life and the value of our inner child. I hope to share my experiences and what I've learned from others when free from judgement. I am not here to judge, for that is for a higher power of our universe.

I am here to remember the child within and to bring it back to my world of business. To respect my own time and to share it with those who are important in my life. To find the laughter, fun, curiosity, adventure, creativity, learning, growth, imagination, emotion and the honesty of the child in all the environments I may touch.

The first thing in life to recognise and to understand is that old saying: "Life is difficult" and when you accept that statement as a fact of life, things will get easier for you. What needs to be understood is that not only is life difficult, but what you require in life is commitment, discipline and determination if you are going to change any aspect of your world. To be honest with others, you must first be honest with yourself. If you are not honest within, then what are you? The most important thing you own in life is your personal character, so look after it well.

You start to build your character from the moment you are born. It is my hope that as you read this book, some of the points resonate with you. I hope that you have the commitment, discipline, and determination, to make the changes you know you should. Whatever the current situation is in your life, maybe you are very happy with what you have, or you may be hating your job and workplace, or you're living in a difficult relationship, or dealing with health or financial issues, or searching for who you are, where you are spiritually. Taking the first step and making a decision to take action to make a change in your life, is the right place to start. If any aspect of your life is hurting, until you decide to change the hurt will remain. I believe the hard lessons in our life will continue to occur, until it hurts so much that changing where we are now is the only course for us to grow. Taking no action at all means we stay as we are, in a place that is killing our growth, and we will die before we discover who we were to become.

The sad thing is, lots of people don't even start to look. From the moment we are conceived we have this innate mechanism to drive our ability to discover who we are. How do we learn to master all this special internal machinery we are born with and to navigate our way through life? To achieve what we are here to achieve and to leave a part of ourselves behind like the plants and animals do, a part that betters the world for those that will follow? The answer for me is by listening to our child within.

> *"Why was your mind given to you, but to think things out for yourself" –*
> *Eleanor Roosevelt*

My goal is to keep the messages contained in this book simple and hopefully provide you with tools to use in your own way. I have always found if you keep it simple one gets the message more quickly. Think things out for yourself. As you read through the chapters I would strongly suggest that you take time to consider where you are right now in your world. Please question any elements where you feel I am suggesting or telling you what to do. Make up your own mind and take away the elements that will make a difference in your life. Learning to question and seeking to understand your own world is vital to your growth. Things may never be as they seem, so always question. Remember it is always up to YOU.

Consider the headings below.

What is life like now for you with your:

- ✓ Health?
- ✓ Relationships – (all)?
- ✓ Career – workplace?
- ✓ Development – (personal or spiritual)?
- ✓ Finance?

We often hear, "try and keep your working life separate from your personal life." Remember, every day you carry your emotions and feelings in both these worlds. I have come across many individuals who stay in the work environment later each day rather than going home. As it is in the workplace that they feel they receive the recognition they desire. This has serious effects on your home life and your family's well-being. This may be you, but if not, I am sure you may know individuals for which this is the case. Living in the false belief that it's the job that keeps them at work and the pressure of the work culture, versus their desire for personal recognition or even just to be heard.

Connecting your work and home relationships will improve the harmony in your life. Allowing discussions in your life to provide for real family time. Allowing your family to call you on your shit when needs be. We find it too easy to make excuses that it's others, who have the control over us and we blame the work culture for keeping us at work. If this is the case for you, ask yourself the question a child would ask, **why?** If you don't like your work environment or home environment, what part are you playing in the survival of these cultures? Remember your company loves you until the restructure. Your spouse/partner loves you romantically until the divorce. You play a part in your contribution to both these environments.

Happiness in your work will spill over into your personal life and vice-versa. Throughout the chapters of this book, I have tried to share my own experiences by bringing back into focus, the child behaviours and questioning skills of a child, such as: **"Why?"** We need to ask **why** more often. We need to decide to take personal responsibility and make the changes we know we must make in our lives. It is never too late to start asking **why**.

It is strange how we are born into this world as a person but somehow, we die with the title of something else. The old saying: "You were born a person and you died a baker." Some box or profession that people have pigeonholed you into. Expectations of a lifestyle or behaviours that you should adhere to. While, the only person that really knows who you are, is you. People may describe you in terms of a brother, sister, mother, father, banker, solicitor/lawyer, carpenter, plumber, as gentle, kind, a miser. As teenagers say, "whatever". These are labels we are given.

Ask yourself, who are you really?

How would you like to be described by others?

Once you've answered this question, then work on becoming this person if you are not already there. Seek the support of your inner child. It is there waiting to be asked.

I dislike when I am in a group of people for the first time and the first question I get is: "What do you do?" Immediately you are placed in a box or given a label of some type. A child will ask your name and do you want to play.

Accepting you for who you are. As you are playing, the next questions may be where you are from/live? Getting to know the authentic you, and building trust. What is important is to find out about the person by asking them to tell you a little about themselves? So let's play and learn from one another and forget the boxes or labels that have been attached to us. Next time you are in the company of others try asking some different questions, like: "what is your favourite colour or music?" or, "beside your work life what do you enjoy doing?"

"I am the father of three boys, I am a brother to five others in my family, I am a friend to many, I am the lover of one and I am a child at heart. I love to write, tell stories and enjoy the craic. My favourite colours are blue, yellow pink and white."

Forget the job labels, they are not important. Get to know the authentic person and you will grow and respect one another for what you each bring to that moment in time. Let's play.

To start, it is important to look at a definition of the word **WORK** – supplied on Google:

Activity involving mental or physical effort done in order to achieve a purpose or result.

"he was tired after a day's work in the fields"
> labor, toil, slog, drudgery, exertion, effort, industry, service;
> More

"synonyms":
> informal grind, sweat, elbow grease;
>
> literary travail
>
> "a day's work in the fields"

Now, let's look at a definition of the word **PLAY**

Engage in activity for enjoyment and recreation rather than a serious or practical purpose.

"the children were playing outside"

amuse oneself, entertain oneself,
enjoy oneself, have fun; More
relax, occupy oneself, divert
oneself

"synonyms":

frolic, frisk, romp, caper;
informal mess around
"Aidan and Robert were playing
with their toys"

No wonder most people dislike their jobs with words like *toil, slog, drudgery.* Which would you prefer in your life? How can we turn our everyday work into fun and play – something we enjoy rather than slog and drudgery? Let us start as we mean to continue. Throughout this book I have inserted pages for you to make your own notes or to draw pictures or doodle – do what you wish. Colour outside the lines, scribble as you will. Bring that child back from within, have fun and play.

"Youth is happy because it has the capacity to see beauty. Anyone who keeps the ability to see beauty never grows old." —Franz Kafka

When I tutor in project management or hold an initial meeting with a new team, I bring a small cuddle toy with me into the class or meeting. This toy usually has some chocolate or sweets attached. I place the toy on the desk or table close to me for all to see and I say nothing about it.

If nobody asks me what its significance is during the class or meeting, I remove it and take it home. When somebody asks about the toy I explain why it is there.

Its significance reminds me of three important points, they are: -

- We should always be curious;
- We should always address the elephant in the room;
- We should state the obvious when we are reviewing documents, financials figures or are presented with a business proposition. I would say: "State the bleeding obvious".

You would be very surprised how often this toy will be removed by me without having received one question as to its significance. The first thing a child would do is, stare directly at the toy and ask about it. It is a shame that in the current school system we learn not to ask why and curiosity is very quickly removed from us, remember the *"phrase curiosity killed the cat"*.

Michael J. Gelb in his book *How to think like Leonardo da Vinci* talks about *The Seven Da Vincina Principles*. Principle 3 is, **Senazione** – the continual refinement of the senses, especially sight, as the means to enliven experience. Gelb goes on to say that, Senazione – focuses on sharpening the senses, consciously. Leonardo believed that refining sensory awareness was the key to enriching experience. As you sharpen your senses, probe the depths of experience, and awaken your childlike powers of questioning, you will encounter increasing uncertainty and ambiguity.

"Adults are just obsolete children and the hell with them." - Dr. Seuss

"Childhood is not from birth to a certain age and at a certain age. The child is grown, and puts away childish things. Childhood is the kingdom where nobody dies." — Edna St. Vincent Millay

And they were bringing children to him that he might touch them, and the disciples rebuked them. But when Jesus saw it, he was indignant and said to them, "Let the children come to me; do not hinder them, for to such belongs the kingdom of God. Truly, I say to you, whoever does not receive the kingdom of God like a child shall not enter it." And he took them in his arms and blessed them, laying his hands on them.
(Mark 10:13-16 ESV)

"A father gives his child nothing better than a good education. "(Quran)

"Every one of you is a protector and guardian and responsible for your wards and things under your care and a man is a guardian of his

family members, and is accountable for those placed under his charge". (Bukhari and Muslim)

Most of these words above were written by a man. In all the holy books the child is cherished and respected for the child is demanded. The holy book you may follow if any, is your choice. The attitude that you bring to wherever you may work is your choice. No matter where you work or no matter how boring or exciting you feel your job may be, there is a difference between you as a person and the job role and postion title you hold. You can decide how you will show up each day, **to work** or **to play.**

I decided in 2000 to leave a secure job where I held a directorship position. I was paid extremely well, but was unhappy with the deceit of the new cultural environment. For me, in the later 3 years I worked in a very toxic environment. Some new and very senior individuals stated that they held one value, yet behaved to the contrary. It was my decision to take control of my future and create and seek a working environment that would allow people to play and collaborate as one team with integrity that encouraged personal learning growth that included fun and balance to one's life.

"The privilege of a lifetime is being who you are." - **Joseph Campbell**

"Never lose the child within you as you grow through your journey of life"

Chapter One

What Direction Are You Heading?

When Alice from the novel *Alice's Adventures in Wonderland* written by Lewis Carroll comes across the Cheshire Cat. The conversation goes as follows: -

Cheshire Puss,' [Alice] began, rather timidly, as she did not at all know whether it would like the name: however, it only grinned a little wider. `Come, it's pleased so far,' thought Alice, and she went on. `Would you tell me, please, which way I ought to go from here?'

That depends a good deal on where you want to get to,' said the Cat.

'I don't much care where' – said Alice.

Then it doesn't matter which way you go,' said the Cat.

1

–so long as I get SOMEWHERE,' Alice added as an explanation.

Oh, you're sure to do that,' said the Cat, `if you only walk long enough.'

Ask your inner child, do you know what direction you are heading?

Do you know your inner child?

The definitions given for the words 'child' or 'Children' may have slightly different slants that all come back to the same meaning. I love the definition 'child – person between birth and full growth, boy or girl'. When do we ever stop growing in our life? I believe never, for what is not growing is decaying; therefore, by definition we are always children. When asked, do I have children, I reply – yes. When I tell their ages, the response is: "You have grown up children?"

I am sure you have heard, the saying such as the children of Israel, or the children of Edom referring to the descendants of a nation or tribe,

2

community, or land. Yet we seem to be forced to lose our childlike qualities as we move through life and age because our appearance may change as we age, but we are always children within. In today's world, we seem to move much more closely to displaying our child qualities in our older years, having grown and gained experiences in life. In reflection, we revert to becoming less tolerant of stupidity and we are not prepared to put up with situations and conditions that do not serve our growth in life. The grumpy old man or crazy old lady scenario? Well, I feel that this is an expression of frustration from not having allowed ourselves to embrace the child within each of us during our 20's, 30's 40's and 50's.

What you create in your life will either support or hinder you in what you want to achieve. By being alive inside, and through our learning, we can create the changes that we need, so we can grow. If we are not willing to learn we do not grow in life, when we are not growing we die. Like a child, it is important to stay curious about the world, to learn and grow each moment and to keep your life simple so that you stay present and aware. Like a child, imagination allows us to see the possibilities that can be – allow your imagination to be released out into your world.

Your thoughts are your worst enemy and your best ally, for it is from them that you will grow or die. They hold your greatest fears and the possibility of creating a gift for all generations to come. Unleash the innocence of that child that lives within you and learn how to focus your thoughts on who you are meant to be. Continue to remind yourself each day, there is only one of you here in the now.

Decide where you want to play in life. Determine what it looks and feels like to be in your playground. Like the culture that is created within an organisation you have the choice to participate within it, change it, or move away from it. Everyone, including you, has a part to play in the organisational culture in which you work. For the culture within the workplace can make the company great, or destroy it.

Creating a culture of respect within a society, community, workplace or home environment encourages you to accept your responsibility in the part that you play. You will either add to a respectful culture or take away from its formation. Each day, you will do this by the actions and thoughts that you bring with you into the environments you touch.

Why do we lose the child within us when we enter the world of business? Why do we try to eliminate it from its culture? Our work environment has a context which it can take strength from for when we show up elsewhere. When our work and personal lives are forced into separation it has its consequences. They are all connected, each feeding off the other to support our journey of growth. Happiness is in the here and now, hoping for your happiness in the future is not achievable, as you are always living in the present. Hoping that things will get better in the future for your business will not produce results unless you actively act in the now. How is that we struggle with taking action in our business decisions when we know it's the right thing to do? You can decide to change how you play the game. You can choose the direction in which you want to go. You can set an intention for your day and the environments in which you will touch.

The question you may ask is **how** can I do this? A better initial question is **why** is it important for me to be happy in my life? I suggest you start with creating this mindset and your *how can I* will come easier.

My suggestion is to consider the following six steps that are within your own control to work through the 'your how can I and how to'.

1. Turn your obsession into your passion.

2. Focus on your passion, get rid of what is distracting you from following it and gain greater clarity on what you want to achieve.

3. Work hard to create consistency in your actions and behaviours. – It does not happen overnight without effort and there may be some failures along the way.

4. Learning to grow – read 20-30 pages of a book per day.

5. Reward yourself continually on achieving success; give yourself a gift – you can decide on how small or big it will be.

6. Support others with your success – give back and mentor where you can. Network with others and remember it's not all about what you might learn, it might be about what others learn from you.

Your responsibilities in life change to developing yourself, so you can be there as the person you are for your family and friends. The care free qualities of the child within does not mean that you are careless in your actions. It does not mean you should shed your responsibilities in life. It does mean changing your mindset as to how you behave towards others. The inner child is naturally caring and concerned with the well-being of others. The spoiled and bold child only learns from the examples and actions of their parents.

Play like that child within and bring it forward in your life. Choose to be that happy child. Follow your inner direction and seek to bring the child within to your place of work. Learn to play again and be that child who understands that when situations and emotions have clarity they become simple to understand and apply in your world.. The one who learns when they are having fun. The one who is free to speak their mind and build honesty as a key value in their life.

What direction are you heading?

My page for notes, scribbles, drawing or doodling

What is one thing I will do next?

My page for notes, scribbles, drawing or doodling

What direction are you heading?

"Believe in yourself and your dreams"

Chapter Two

The Savvy Child Within You

We all have a savvy inner child within us; some forgotten forever, but never lost. It is important to seek out our inner child and switch on the qualities it brings to our lives and in this world, from our birth to our death. There are those whom wish to kill off that child within us for it does not serve their purpose.

When we enter our working environments, cultures and activities they remove elements of our personalities, especially the child within us. Work seems to provide no place for your inner child. Such as, honesty, curiosity, imagination, fun, laughter, friendship, emotion or spirited adventures. Even though that excitement is within you, your business

13

world can stifle its presence. Remember when you dreamt and aimed for high achievements, you knew what you wanted to be when you grew up.

What we wanted as a child in our lives might be poles apart from what we end up doing in our business world. Many of us fall into a career path as the opportunity arises or out of necessity. When do you recall learning the most? For me, it was always when I was having fun and enjoying what I was doing in my personal and business world. The attributes of a child support our growth and development. Why are they so absent in our business world? We have the choice to bring our childlike qualities into this environment. Accepting that they have a place and then having the personal courage to display them. We live in a world of being concerned about what others think of us, or what society has accepted as the norm. We need to believe in ourselves and display our inner feelings as a child would do, without worrying what others may think of us. Start by laughing out loud more, be it in your work place, or personal interactions on a bus or a train journey.

> *The most important ingredients in a child's education are curiosity, interest, imagination and a sense of adventure of Life – Eleanor Roosevelt – You Learn by Living*

These child ingredients are lifelong supports to our growth. What I have personally found helpful, is to be who you know you are, don't try and run with individuals that take away from your growth. Hang out with people who can support you in growing and add to your well-being. As a child we may have been influenced by the wrong people, those whom we thought were our friends. Remember, learning is sent to us in different forms to support our growth in both the now and later in life. Respect what you have learned from the past and take responsibility for your part in both the good and bad. Looking back can feel like regret, looking forward is the better option as we can't change our past, only our future which is yet to arrive. The now is what is important. Going forward, get rid of the so-called friends and work colleagues you don't need and pick your true friends well.

Growing happens when we take personal responsibility for the changes we want to make in our world; change is in your hands. The business world will act to discourage you from bringing and expressing childlike qualities in the workplace. I would encourage you to be brave. It is okay to be scared, but don't be afraid of doing something new and unfamiliar.

Why do we work? Is it really for the money? Yes, we get money for our labour, because that is how the economy works in today's world. Money may not be the only way of the future. We seek engagement with others, to be inspired and to make a contribution in what we do. How can we ensure that we have a chance to deliver on these aspirations when our natural child qualities are discouraged? Every avenue we are directed down is driven by the focus of earning money. By using money as the goal, we are shackled to the control and imprisonment of a work environment that we end up hating. We are educated to work under the culture of having a boss, working for a corporate or organisational entity, rather than with people. We don't play under someone, we play with them. Look at the Ubuntu movement way of life which supports the collaboration and contribution of all in the delivery of what we need in life. Looking out for each other.

Description

Ubuntu (/ʊˈbuːntʊ/ uu-boon-tuu; Zulu pronunciation: [ùɓúntʼú])[1][2] is a Nguni Bantu term roughly translating to *"human kindness"*. [dubious – discuss] It is an idea from the Southern African region which means literally "human-ness", and is often translated as "humanity towards others", but is often used in a more philosophical sense to mean "the belief in a universal bond of sharing that connects all humanity"- (*Source* -Wikipedia, the free encyclopaedia)

I am sure there are moments in your life where you may have witnessed mean and cruel children. They are often educated by the actions of their parents, teachers and social environments. In my opinion, they are taught by disgruntled adults who have lost their own inner child and human values of respect for themselves and others. For some, the environment in which they grew up may not have been a very happy one and they have carried these feelings into their adult life. Finding their inner child can be difficult for some. But the goodness of the savvy child is there waiting for you to seek it out.

We know we are savvy, remember as children we played together, shared together, laughed together and looked out for each other even in difficult times, so why not now?

> *"There can be no keener revelation of a society's soul than the way in which it treats its children."* - Nelson Mandela

My page for notes, scribbles, drawing or doodling

What is one thing I will do next?

My page for notes, scribbles, drawing or doodling

"If you want to change your behaviour, change your point of view"

Chapter Three

Fun & Laughter

Even the word laughter brings a smile to my face. When was the last time you had a good belly laugh? Did you ever laugh with someone when you were in a place where it was not appropriate to laugh? When I did this, I would almost wet myself trying to hold in the laughter. On a few occasions, I could feel I was about to wee myself. Tears would run down my face and I might even have had a pain in my side from laughing so much. I can picture back to incidents with my older sister Maggie, as we very often got into real trouble from laughing in places on occasions when we were not supposed to. Trying to hold it back and the tears running down our faces as we shuck, pinching each other to try and make it stop.

Once in a management meeting, where all of the executives were senior to my position, the Chairman of the organisation was present, so every director was on their best behaviour and one could feel the tension in the room. That unmentioned rule between the directors, "you don't have a go at me and I won't have a go at you in front of the Chairman". Both a colleague and I were making a presentation on training within the organisation, it was all very serious stuff. When my colleague was presenting the Chairman passed me a handwritten note. I could not read his writing, so I wrote back "you are in the wrong job, can't read your handwriting you should have been a doctor" and I slipped the piece of paper back to him. The Chairman burst out laughing and read my comments to the rest of the board. The whole atmosphere in the meeting changed and the room felt relaxed. This opened the door for more fun, laughter and a more positive mood overshadowed the meeting. Afterwards both my colleague and I received very positive comments about our presentation and they indicated they enjoyed the meeting. What was important to us was that we achieved a commitment and gained support for our business proposal.

I was recently reminded, during a discussion around working with individuals who have very positive attitude and who bring fun into the workplace, that when you look at children playing, they are always laughing. As we get older, we seem to lose this sense of fun and laughter within us, especially in the workplace. Everything becomes *'serious stuff'*. As if there is something not right with laughing out loud. Are we not supposed to have fun in what we do? How do you feel when you hear or see people laughing? I know I feel I would like to be part of that discussion or meeting.

A study conducted at the University of Maryland Medical Center in the USA linked laughter and the healthy function of blood vessels. In 2005, researchers presented that laughter causes dilation of the inner lining of blood vessels the endothelium and increases blood flow. When we laugh the brain releases endorphins which can relieve some physical pain. It also produces a number of antibody producing cells that enhance the effectiveness of T-cells, which in turn strengthens the immune system. In 2016, an article written on healthy lifestyles from the Mayo Clinic USA, stated that laughter can: *'Activate and relieve your stress response. A rollicking laugh fires up and then cools down your stress response, and it can increase your heart rate and blood pressure. The result? A good, relaxed feeling'.*

I'm sure you have heard the saying that *'laughter is the best medicine'*. The best time to try it out is now. So smile – go on smile, even if it feels forced. Once you start you will begin to giggle. How are you feeling? Muscles a little less tense, less stressed, mood changing? Go ahead and have a good old laugh. There is another short laughing exercise at the end of this chapter that I would encourage you to try.

Every day I have a good old laugh with my partner and friends. If only at some of the silliest things we might say to each other. Laughter is the food of good health and the opening of the mind for good thoughts and ideas. Lots of the posts shared on Facebook are jokes and funny animal videos. So when you hear – a comment like, "this is no laughing matter" and you feel like laughing, ask: "WHY not?" Often understanding the funny side of a situation will support you in finding the answers to the issue at hand. Often when we look back at situations in business we laugh about them.

To all the owners of a company, the CEO's, Managing Directors and Managers, whatever position you hold; I would encourage you to consistently bring laughter to your business. Too often, when the boss appears out of their office, all laugher and funs stops. Why does this happen? Is it fear? Children don't stop laughing because an adult appears in the room, in fact they laugh more. Sometimes so much that the adult cannot help but join in on the laughter. The worries or issues that the adult may have had seem to just disappear, if only for a short time. Thus allowing the opportunity for clearer thoughts, which in turn could bring a solution to whatever the worrying issue may have been about. Is it because we believe the boss may feel if we are enjoying ourselves we are not working? I had more fun carrying out my work when I was having a good old laugh doing it. Sometimes, if I was to try and explain the situation or comments to an outsider, it may not make any sense or they may not see the humour. I still start to smile and laugh. We have all used the phrase "you needed to be there to understand" – so go ahead and create more of those situations for laughter in your workplace.

Bringing laughter and fun into one's working life can be the health for the soul of a business. Laughter stirs up creativity and can stimulate solutions to business issues. Don't you want to be connected to those teams in your workplace that seem to laugh a lot? There is one thing about the Irish that is, they have a great sense of humour and the ability to joke and laugh, especially at themselves.

Try this daily exercise - pretend for one moment that you are starting your car on a very cold frosty morning and use the sound of laughter to simulate the noise of the engine trying to turnover. Laugh from that place of the inner child within you. As I have heard it said, a fart held in, travels up through the body and into the brain where shitty ideas come from. A good old laugh held in, gives you a pain in the stomach where all those good gut instincts are held; so let them out and laugh more. Start every day with a laugh and make someone smile today.

> *Two Irish friends are sitting on the side of the harbour looking out to sea, watching some scuba divers in a small boat. One friend turns to the other and asks, "why do they always fall backwards out of the boat." To which his friend replied," if they fell forwards they would still be in the fecking boat."*

The most sophisticated people I know - inside

they are all children." –

Jim Henson

MEL WITH TRIXIE THE CLOWN

BRINGING FUN INTO YOUR WORLD

PHOTOGRAPHER – SELINA MORRISON

MANY THANKS

TRIXIE THE CLOWN

(AKA -CHARMAINE MIRON)

WWW.SILLYOFTHEVALLEY.COM

PHOTOGRAPHER

SELINA MORRISON

WWW.SELINAPHOTOGRAPHY.CA

"The secret of genius is to carry the spirit of childhood into maturity." - Thomas Huxely

My page for notes, scribbles, drawing or doodling

What is one thing I will do next?

My page for notes, scribbles, drawing or doodling

BIG SMILE FOR YOU

Chapter Four

Honesty & Transparency

"Whoever can be trusted with very little can also be trusted with much, and whoever is dishonest with very little will also be dishonest with much". Luke 16:10

"In Islam, honesty implies maintaining sincerity and truthfulness in all actions, interactions, and transactions, and the issue of honesty touches almost all aspects of human life."

There is no such thing as a white lie. Either something is true or not true. What is often found to be missing in the world of most personal and business relationships is pure honesty. We are taught from an early age to lie and by whom? Our elders and yes, our parents. There is a saying: "Out of the mouths of babes" referencing the truth and wisdom of a child. The innocense and brutal honest comment of a child.

37

The child who will call it as they feel or see it without judgement. Remember the story of the *Emperor's New Clothes* written by *Hans Christen Andersen.* As a child, if we did something that was not acceptable to one of our parents and we knew that telling the truth might very quickly get us into trouble, we found it easier to lie. We knew straight away from their tone of voice. We started to associate some elements of pain, fear and punishment with telling the truth. As a child and teenager I told lies. Just one example was to support my father when we would be out together. I would support his excuse for his lateness home to my mother with whatever excuse he provided. As a teenager I lied at times to both my parents as to where I was going and what I was up to. Were these lies or were my answers performing to my parents expectations? Were they untruths to protect them from what I was really up to? So, is this the start of what makes it okay to lie and protect people from the real truth?

When we accidently meet some acquaintances on the street or in coffee shops, we exchange pleasantries. To be polite we may suggest meeting up in the future sometime. Even if they are people, that we don't like, and we clearly know that, this is not going to happen. We say and do what we feel the other person wants to hear from us. There seems to be this false pretense about the situation. We take this attitude into our relationships and work environments. A child might say straight out: *"I don't want to play with you anymore."* When was the last time you were dishonest or lied in your relationship, to a client or to your work colleagues or you partner?

Within organizations, many people seem to be missing the ability to be honest. A common phrase used in the workplace is: "To be honest with you" or "if I were honest with you". During all the other discussions you had were they being dishonest with you? We expect honesty in the workplace. We expect honesty in relationships. We expect honesty from our leaders. We expect honesty from our governments. We expect honesty from the banking, legal and investment sectors. Now I am reflecting on the previous chapter and having a good old laugh as we have seen this not to be true from any of these sectors.

It is very rare to find honesty in any of the above-mentioned places. Let us hope that we deliver and find honesty in our personal relationships because these are the ones that really matter in life. Does the company that you work for really care and appreciate you? I have said this previously; Your company loves you until the organisational restructure.

As a child, we are compliant to our parents' expectations and in business we are compliant to the stock markets, our bosses and or the required company's lies. There are excellent examples all around us of business dishonesty and lying to, clients, shareholders and the markets. A few to mention are Anglo Irish Bank and Enron and who knows the full truth of the political and government involvement in both. To mention only two items of countless dishonest activities: Anglo Irish Bank senior directors and chairman knowingly provided inaccurate figures for eight consecutive years on directors' loans. Along with other controversial financial transactions with Irish Life & Permanent meant to mispresent their year-end financial accounts. Simon Carswell's book titled ***Anglo Republic: Inside the Bank that Broke Ireland*** is an excellent read which demonstrates the greed and corruption through dishonesty. In Ireland it is now, nearly ten years on that we are seeing the fines and prison sentences being imposed; with some reluctance, I must say. It is shocking to witness the length of sentences issued for the results of these crimes in comparison to the sentences handed down for lesser crimes which had less impact on a population. The shedding of evidence to support their crimes and who actually has something or some hold over someone else that will turn the other way; rather than deliver rightful justice. In the USA, Enron's scandalous financial activities lead to its bankruptcy and the loss of billons in pensions and share prices. Corruption breeds corruption it can force an individual who was not corrupt to be dishonest; as the only way of surviving at that point in time. Having to protect themselves from additional harm.

Institutional accountability for their dishonest actions such as corporations, the

42

banking system and governments, is very soon swept away and forgotten. It becomes business as usual for them. One side is seeking to win and the other side must lose. Look at our political institutions, especially the current major world powers.

> *"What is true is that honesty is incompatible with the amassing of a large fortune"* Mahatma Gandhi

Respectful working environments encourage honesty and it is a must if one wants to experience good personal relationships. If you were to ask a friend, work colleague or your partner would they want you to be honest with them no matter what? I believe the majority of us would say yes. In my personal opinion, there are two types of lies, lies to others and lies to yourself. Ask yourself this question, if I were to be honest with both myself and others from this moment forward would my life be better?

What is the fear that we have that is stopping us from being totally honest with others and ourselves? Remember the line from the movie *A Few Good Men: "You can't handle the truth"*. Some believe that these words are correct. It is not for you or the person who is being honest to worry about how it will be perceived or handled. How a person reacts or feels is their issue to deal with, not yours. The phrase *"sometimes the truth hurts"* is correct: We often have images of ourselves or a different picture of the situation. How we respond to the truth is up to us and nobody else. We can either respond positively by thanking the person for informing us and for their honesty. Or we can react negatively by either attacking the person or others because of what you have heard. Knowing and using the truth in a positive or negative way can be supportive or harmful. We all own 100% of our behaviour. The truth is often withheld only for the benefit of others to gain from it. In this way one party benefits while others may lose out. One exception may be if you tell the truth in a given situation it could directly lead to the physical harm of others. If you think it's wrong in your mind then it is wrong, but only you can decide how to act.

It is a good idea to take time to think before you act when you hear a truth that might stir up a lot of emotion within you. When we act emotionally we sometimes act irrationally. Then again, we are emotional beings built to react to life's situations. We have feelings that need to be acknowledged. When you are being honest with yourself or someone else, consider the intention of your action. The intention of your inner child is to face reality as you feel it.

By being honest surely our intention is not to hurt ourselves or others. This might be true, but this is not always the case as the truth is often used to hurt others. If we were more supportive of each other or challenged each other to be the best we can be, then telling the truth or being truthful with ourselves would be much easier. Carefully consider the actions that you demonstrate to support the other person when you are being honest with them?

Make a commitment to yourself that you will be honest and tell the truth for at least the next 48 hours, if not longer or always. Try and do this no matter what questions you are asked or how you may feel about a situation and then reflect on how easy or difficult you find this task. You may think this is easy, but the reality is that most people will fail within the first few hours. It's a shame that the majority of people will find it very difficult to be truly honest as to how they feel about a situation or with others for at least a 48-hour period. What happens is, we decide that it's only a white lie. This is the best excuse we can come up with. Worst of all, not even being truly honest with ourselves does not allow us to grow in the moment. Even if you were alone for this period, would you be able to be honest with yourself and take action to make a change in your life?

I heard a story of an elderly man being interviewed by a younger interviewer – the interviewer asked the elderly man, what he felt his weakest quality might be. The old man replied, *"honesty"*. The young interviewer responded that he did not think honesty was a weakness. To which the old man replied: *"I don't really give a shit what you think."*

Would you say that all politicians or the leaders of our countries tell the truth? – This too makes me laugh when I ask myself this question. Would it be a good thing for society if the only option for politicians was to always tell the truth? Most definitely yes, regardless of the circumstances. Will this ever happen every time they speak? I believe not, even never. Now I am dreaming or living in coo coo land. That said, circumstances and nature have the ability to bring about change.

Like the characters in *A Few Good Men*, most politicians assume that the public "can't handle the truth", and so they decide what we should and should not know. The word "spin" is commonly used to inform the public as to what is happening, but it is another excuse used to tell lies. The justification used for control over a population. The next time a political candidate knocks on your door looking for your vote, ask them if it is their practice to and will they commit to always tell the truth? Ask them if they have they lied in the past and watch their response. What do you think it will be?

I can hear all the arguments from politicians for why sometimes it's best not to tell the truth – my response is: "It's not okay to not tell the truth". But yet it happens and we excuse ourselves by believing it's best to lie. Again, masked as a white lie – well as I have said before it's either true or not. It is the interests of a few which are protected by politicians for their own survival and personal interests. It is ironic that Politicians call for transparency. Yes, there are some excellent and mostly truthful politicians, the big issue is they don't survive within their own environment. They suffocate within themselves and leave frustrated as their honest efforts to do good fade. They are often persecuted by the public for their honesty, as they are saying everything is NOT rosy in the garden and they tell it as it is. Their environment often forces the good politicians to lie to survive.

Until they personally reach their own point of self-respect, dignity and value of integrity.

What is important is how we express the truth and the way we approach the situation or person. It is not our right to decide how one should handle or react to the truth. Our inner fears of how we might be seen or thought of by family, friends and colleagues can be an issue when it comes to telling the truth. We may choose to be a people pleaser and take the easy route, mask our lies again with: *"It was only a little white lie so that's okay"*.

> *"what others think of us is none of our business what we think of ourselves is our business"* – *Stephen Hopson.*

If we are honest with ourselves then we should not care what others think of us. If we are honest with ourselves then we can start to change or do something about the situation we may be in. The first step is to always be truthful with oneself. The second step is to make the changes you know you must and the third step is to continue to be truthful for the rest of your life without intentionally causing hurt and harm to yourself or others.

> *"A faithful friend is the medicine of life."*
> *-The Apocrypha, 6:16*

When we talk about making the changes in our lives that we need, too often individuals will equate this to being financially successful in some form within the workplace. We measure ourselves against other people or other material things people have in their lives. The pressure we place ourselves under to achieve success. So, who decides what the measurements of success are in your life?

Is your measurement of success having lots of money?

Is it being very famous?

What is it for you?

What about a measure of embracing that happy child within?

Be careful what you are choosing to measure your success against. I would ask you to consider this question for yourself carefully as your measures are for you only.

> *"To thine own self be true,"* -
> Polonius. - William Shakespeare -
> Hamlet

Inner happiness and peace of mind are more important than trying to compete for foolish accolades. We often don't realise, what we have right before our eyes and fail to appreciate the simple values and things that are given to us in life for free. I have read many times that you must seek what you love doing and keep doing it. Never a truer phrase. The difficulty is coming to terms with what you really want and taking that leap of faith into, sometimes, the unknown. A few phrases I have used are realize "What floats your boat?" or "What makes your eyes light up and sparkle?"

What is your passion?

There is right and wrong; there is no in between. There is honesty; it is either true or it is not? Don't fool yourself, for it is only you whom you are fooling. Yes, there are different perspectives – and we believe what is the truth to us – but we are not talking about perspectives we are talking about honesty in anyone's language.

I was once taught a very important lesson from the honesty of my partner. We were having lunch at a restaurant in Sinina, a small town north of Bucharest in early 2007. A young man approached the table and left some articles for sale with a small note saying he was deaf and by purchasing one of these items it would support him. I had experienced this in other towns and cities in Europe, and on several occasions paid little attention at the time. When I looked at the items placed on this table I could see no value in them for me. The young man was not having luck selling his items to anyone else in the restaurant. No one gave him any recognition. When the restaurant owner saw the young man, he proceeded to have him removed from the premises. When we finished our lunch and left the restaurant, the young man was still outside hanging around. I put my hand in my pocket and gave him a few Romanian Lei. The young man offered me some of the items, which I refused to accept. I wanted to give him the money. What a fool I was, I never made conversation with him, I never really acknowledged him. I acted the big man that was able to hand him money. My partner asked me, why I had not accepted any of the man's wares. I replied: "He can sell them again to someone else and I had no value for them." My partner asked, "but what about the value of what this young man was doing? "If he wanted to beg, he could have begged from you, but he didn't. He was working and selling his items." I thanked my partner for this lesson. If you have people around you that will point out opportunities for you to learn and grow, you are a very lucky person.

In our working environment or personal life, we often surround ourselves with individuals who will not point out our failures and therefore, we miss these vital opportunities to grow and learn. Find those people who only want the best for your growth in this world and learn with them. They are your friends. It's not always about you learning it can go both ways.

*A friend is one that knows you as you
are, understands where you have been,
accepts what you have become, and
still, gently allows you to grow.
William Shakespeare*

Honesty and transparency are virtues of strength in your life - never mistake honesty in yourself or others as a weakness. Find your inner child who knows and calls it as they feel it. See your core values and live by them.

Research Johari Window and seek out the unknown self.

Nobody likes a liar, as our inner child would say – *liar, liar pants on fire!*

My page for notes, scribbles, drawing or doodling

What is one thing I will do next?

My page for notes, scribbles, drawing or doodling

Chapter Five

How Children Communicate

We should all learn to communicate like children – they communicate with great feelings and their full emotions. Watch a child get excited or when they get sad their facial expressions say it all. As we grow older we seem to lose the ability to connect with, and display our emotions externally. The result is that as we grow, we live in our external world and lose our internal world of questioning who we are. We abandon that part of our essential emotional growth behind. Our business world is where we learn to operate and it becomes our reality, losing that child within.

Definition – Feelings *an emotional state or reaction. "a feeling of joy" Synonyms love, affection, fondness, tenderness, warmth, warmness, emotion, sentiment; - the emotional side of* *someone's character; emotional responses or tendencies to respond. **a belief**, especially a vague or irrational one. "he had the feeling that he was being watched" **Synonyms** suspicions, sneaking suspicion, notion, inkling, hunch, funny feeling, feeling in one's bones, fancy, idea. An opinion, typically one shared by several people. "a feeling grew that justice had not been done" **Synonyms** opinion, belief, view, impression, intuition, instinct, hunch, estimation, guess. "my feeling is that it is true."*

Communication on all levels is vital to our development. In every one of our communications we are expressing, through feelings, one or several of the above synonyms; we are always communicating. In our relationships, family, community, work environments and in our society. When we fail to communicate that something is wrong or not right in our lives, we fail ourselves and often others. In business, for example, failure to communicate one's understanding of a position, their feelings or point of view continues to leave it unclear and open to misunderstanding. It is vital that we try and communicate a clear understanding of our feelings and position on a subject, be that positive or negative. The child within you has no hesitation in letting their feelings be known, watch a child throw a wobbler in a shop. Watch a child's face when they are excited or dislike a piece of food. The child within us does not hold back, or contain their emotional voice.

In our business world we ignore our inner feelings from the communication process. Not the child, for it is from the child that we experience the outburst of emotions. It is through communicating these emotions that one can establish a sense of awareness of a position. Have you heard of the saying "Stop acting like a child!"? Don't hide what you really feel. What you feel inside and what you communicate through your verbal, written and body language, speaks out as to who you are. The language we use, how we dress and how we behave will communicate an external message about you.

How we act and behave is very important and speaks volumes to those around you, about who you are. Even if you are totally oblivious to the message you are sending out. I have often said to my work colleagues and friends, "don't rely on what I say, watch how I behave." How we behave in our work place, home, community or country, says a lot about who we are as a person and collectively as an organisation or society.

How would you like to communicate in your relationships with partners, your family and in your workplace? Children always ask the straight questions about themselves such as: "Do you like me?", "do you like playing games with me?" Ask the people in your personal and business life what advice they can give you about your communication style, do they like to be around and play with you?

A sample of four questions:

1. What is one thing you like about how I communicate and how I behave when I am in your company?

2. What would you say are three of my good communication qualities?

3. What would you like to see me doing more of, so that I communicate better with you?

4. What would you like to see me doing less of, so that I communicate better with you?

Choose individuals in your workplace and personal life whose opinion you value and trust. You may be very surprised at the responses. Do you have the courage to ask these questions? Remember it is you who will benefit from the information gained. Make sure that you thank those you have chosen for their time and responses, whether you like, dislike, agree or disagree with what they have told you. What you do with the insights you now have is up to you. Remember this is just a picture of their perceptions of you. If you take what they have said on board and make changes, then the next time you ask them or other individuals, you would hope they have an improved picture of you.

Be aware that we are continually sending out messages which can be misunderstood and sometimes those messages require clarification. The first step: In improving how you communicate is, to have an understanding of your starting place - as you are seen today. The second: To know how you would ideally like to be seen by others. The third step: To make the changes required to support your vision. Presenting a good picture and positive feeling about you is important. Honesty from within yourself and the goodness to do no harm to others, this is all that matters (it's not always about the hokey pokey and you turn around). Over 90% of your behaviour is non-verbal. People only hear a small percentage of what you say, but they see and feel the way you say it. Don't lose the ability to share your feelings as an adult, especially the male population. Seek your inner child, regardless of gender and share your feelings freely, as they will come naturally to you.

Like the child, keep your communications simple and be true to yourself. Many people fail because they fear that if they change their behaviour or, change how they say things, people will not like them anymore and they will be seen as different. They fear they are not good enough. What you say, how you behave towards others communicates who you are from within. It is more important that you like yourself first.

Have a look at your organisation and the statements it makes around its people and clients. Are they just lovely written words; but in reality they mean nothing? Do they actively come alive, and communicate every behaviour throughout the organisation? Often one of the missing communication processes in business is the ability to ask how people really feel. The higher the level of management, the less this seems to happen. Why? because they are fearful of being human. Showing a feeling could be seen as a weakness by others and used against them in some format from within the organisation. Dr Edward DeBono uses a well proven and established process within his critical thinking styles the "feeling hat – the red hat" as he recognised that understanding and sharing emotional feelings supports an organisation.

Once at a senior business meeting the Managing Director, who was several positions my senior, was really coming at me aggressively in the way he was asking questions. I did not understand why, I seemed to be upsetting him. Everyone at the meeting could feel the tension in the room. At one stage I requested a short break from the discussion. I told him I was feeling very uneasy and flustered. I was unable to think straight or respond to his questions accurately. During the break the other participants told me that they could feel the aggression and they felt that it took some courage from me to say what I said. I had this inner child feeling, this is not fun and I do not want to play this game anymore. When the meeting started again the Managing Director apologised, as he did not realise he was making me and others feel very uncomfortable. The rest of the meeting was very productive with some excellent fun in parts.

My experience has been that most organisations fail to genuinely ask, individuals how they are feeling about the topic and discussions taking place during meetings. If asked how they are feeling in a business meeting, most people may not truthfully tell how they really feel. Individuals tend to be in ego mode. Often, people feel that there is no genuine concern in the question and it has only been asked for appearances sake. Only by learning and trusting your gut or, in other words, trusting your "inner child" will you call it as you see it and say how you actually feel.

Communication is the expression of who we are and how we feel within ourselves and with others. One of the most important aspects of communication is the honesty of telling it as it is. We need to ask ourselves and others the right questions. What will make the situation/position different, what **can I** or others do?

Communicate how we feel in life, within our work, with our partner with our family and children. I used to ask my kids when they got back from school how they got on during the day - wrong question. They responded with "fine". Instead, when I asked them how they felt in school, they responded with: "I felt good, I felt happy or I felt bored". This response allowed me to ask more questions, like: "What made you feel happy?" Too often we shy away from asking questions around feelings in the workplace and within our personal relationships. In other words, we have fallen asleep inside and we now operate in robot mode. Try it with your family, friends or colleagues. Ask how they are genuinely feeling about a situation or activity. It's as simple as recognizing situations and asking how someone is feeling. What, if anything, can you do to make them feel differently? Better support or better understanding, the fact that they feel heard or giving them some space to think things through might help them better understand and not feel judged.

In business disputes, before we make judgements, we must try and gain a clear understanding as to where the other party may be coming from, or the position they hold. Understanding the emotion attached to a position is vital to being able to respond effectively.

Change is in your hands and only you can decide how you will communicate within your business and personal life. It takes discipline, commitment, and determination to maintain a change of one's behaviour. Learning how to really communicate with feelings in all aspects of your life takes practice as we grow. Listening without judgement is the best place to start.

Wanting to feel from the gut, your inner child. Life comes to us in stages, and learning to live and accept each stage is important. You can never change what you have done or what has happened to you in the past. You can learn from the past to help shape your future. Only you can make the decision to learn. Nobody else can make it for you.

> *"Don't try and be someone else for everyone else is taken – Oscar Wilde*

Your life is important to you and it has the potential to inspire others through honest communications. Those that you touch in your life will know and feel this, that's all that is important, be it one person or millions of people you will have made a difference. If a friend will not tell you who will? Be someone's friend.

> *"Many people will walk in and out of your life, but only true friends will leave footprints in your heart"- Eleanor Roosevelt*

Change is not difficult, it just feels different. You are unique in the world and you are here to make a difference. When we are children, the world is for us to conquer with our dreams of who we will become. Yet in the business world these dreams are masked and often ridiculed, because we lose that child within us. Don't let this happen to you. Action starts with an emotion to take action, which causes movement in your environment. Motion moves us either backwards or forwards it does not allow you to stand still.

> *We keep moving forward, opening new doors, and doing new things, because we're curious and curiosity keeps leading us down new paths. - Walt Disney*

My page for notes, scribbles, drawing or doodling

What is one thing I will do next?

My page for notes, scribbles, drawing or doodling

Chapter Six

Creating a Safe Playground

Continuing along the topic of, if your best friend won't tell you who will. In the workplace a culture of political games, mistrust, positional jockeying, laziness and the lack of honesty are often very difficult issues to address. It may feel easier sometimes to allow this type of culture to exist and what tends to happen, people turn a blind eye and it gets ignored. You could be leading it, you could be participating in it, you could be ignoring it or you might be at the receiving end of it. Whatever position you are in, you hold a level of responsibility for this culture.

No matter where one works, I am sure that experiencing some elements of unacceptable behaviour is common. The most frequent form of behaviour and reaction of individuals, to a bad culture, is the avoidance of dealing with the issues. Positional power can be used by individuals to continue to ensure that a form of bad culture is maintained because it is self-supporting. To which using positional power is one of the greatest weaknesses in a non-military management structure. That said, even military personnel often misuse their rank and soldiers learn quickly not to follow fools. The child within can become a bully yet its natural inner self dislikes bullies or being made to look foolish.

In business we often reward an individual's behaviour that supports this type of culture and we punish those who stand up against it. Organisations lose good people because they don't know how or what to do to make the required changes. The question they ask themselves is: *"How do I stand up to this bad behaviour?"* Not knowing how, they leave the company. When someone leaves the organization, you will always get the true story over a few pints in the bar or over a coffee. You get the rubbish on the exit interview form, as they don't want to rock the boat. The pay cheque does not buy company loyalty. Remember people leave people not organisations. Nine times out of ten it is because somebody in their workplace is making their lives difficult and unhappy to remain (their boss or colleagues). Or, not having a safe place to play within the workplace. Why is this? Its around the lack of honesty and fear of retribution.

Not knowing how to manage bad behaviour or not having the skills to deal with it. The result is, it is allowed to exist within the organisation. To justify the situation senior management make up false beliefs and statements to hide behind or disguise the real issues. For example: *"This is a tough business and this is how we do things around here, if you can't get with the programme you will not survive, so you better decide, are you with us or against us?"*

This type of environment is rampant in governments and political arenas. An environment is created where individuals are fearful to address the culture or even question it. The fish smells from the head first, who is head of your business? The bully in the school yard is still the same bully in business. Yes, we all have the bold child within us who has never felt heard and is trying its best to get noticed. It would appear that bad or bullying behaviour seems the only course of action that's noticed and heard.

The result: Left unsaid, it usually leads to poor performance, stress, lack of development, emulating behavioural styles, absenteeism, isolation and termination. Environments where political games, lack of trust, positional power and the lack of honesty thrives, can exist in all organizations. A bullying culture thrives well, in sectors like the banking systems, abuse within the legal system, policing, military, Governments and large corporations. Ask the questions as a child would about your workplace: "Is this environment right, fair, respectful and honest? Is this what friends do to each other? Is this an environment where we feel safe in who we are and can play safe together with respect for each other?"

Organisations believe they do what is expected of them. They have all the right policies, the right slogans written somewhere, maybe on the Company walls. Their vision, mission and value statements are created for all to see and read, but seldom are they followed. The issue is that it is very difficult for companies to pay attention to their stated values when it comes to the actual implementation. I am sure you have seen companies with written values regarding customers and employees, yet they continue to actively behave and demonstrate the opposite of what they proclaim.

Many companies have changed the name of the department or section with the responsibility for employees to "people". For some reason they think by changing the name, it will change the way people will perceive them as a company. One of the latest names on the market is *"Human Capital"*. Please, give me a break! I cringe when I hear these department titles.

Who is responsible for people in an organisation? Your Chief Executive Officer (CEO). If the CEO of the company really believes that their people make or break the organisation then it is their responsibility to actively demonstrate through their own actions that this is the case. The CEO must also ensure that all their direct reports behave similarly and so on right throughout the Company. Find out what your CEO's top personal values are. Their real values will be demonstrated in their behaviour and how they treat others. Remember when you were a child there was always this friend whom you looked up to. They were great to be around. You had some great times and adventures exploring with them. They always seemed to have the best ideas and made the games more fun. You knew that if you were in trouble they would listen and you could tell them anything, any secret. You knew it was safe with them. That's what your business leader must demonstrate, a safe place for all to play. Watch if they encourage acts of kindness within the organization.

If the CEO of your workplace is not actively involved with the day to day interests of their people then I would suggest you weigh the pros and cons of staying, or consider whether it is in your best interest to move on. Why, well shit flows downhill and if the top management are speaking and delivering shit, then guess where it will land? If it is your decision to move on to another organisation or to work on your own business, it is a positive move and I would encourage you to strongly consider your options.

If you decide to stay, what do you think happens when someone decides to raise the cultural environment as an issue? Well apart from full denial, here are some of the most common reactions/responses (not in any particular order). You might have experienced one or several of these reactions:

- Delighted that someone has spoken out and called it for what it is.

- Individuals receiving the information can get defensive.

- Shoot and discredit the messenger.

- Individuals agree with the views but are sometimes fearful to be seen to agree in public. They are delighted someone else sees it as they do. But when raised internally in an open forum they will revert back to previous behaviour of denial.

- You get a thank you for raising the issues and agreement that there is some truth in what you say. Then, through behaviour, no action is taken and nothing changes. It only gets worse, especially for the person who raised the issue.

- Then there are those that take the courage – acceptance – and willingness to address the real issues and take action and provide the support where necessary to make changes.

I recall a time when I spoke directly to the CEO of a business regarding a bully on his staff. The dogs on the street knew this senior person's behaviour was both dishonest, aggressive and that they used bullying tactics on both their work colleagues and suppliers. I am sorry to say the CEO did nothing to address the issue and the actions of bullying continued.

If you are experiencing poor behaviour in your organisation then do as a child does: Get upset, scream, bang doors or break something until you get the attention you need. Start acting as they say: "Like a child", because until people stand up and take notice little will change. Change often comes from a little turbulence in one's life. Whatever you do, change is in your hands so, ***never punish honesty in your work***

colleagues (Suggested reading *Crummey Vs Ireland*). At times I think of Mother Nature and how she deals with her environments through bringing about change. Be that slow erosion or by immediate action, often seen as a disaster such as forest fires which ignite naturally to clear the way for younger growth.

Let the child continue to grow within and call it as you see it, as others may not speak out. Use the courage from within to be brave. Think of the playground you want to create where it is safe to play with whom you want to play with.

> *For three hundred years we have had our focus on the individual. We have distinguished him from the objective world as the Middle Ages did not think of doing. We have given him the world and the universe as a playground for exploration and discovery.* - John Grierson

My page for notes, scribbles, drawing or doodling

What is one thing I will do next?

My page for notes, scribbles, drawing or doodling

"People know your name, not your story. They've heard what you've done, but not what you've been through" - Unknown

Chapter Seven

Our Inner Teacher

"You have to grow from the inside out. None can teach you, none can make you spiritual. There is no other teacher but your own soul."
-Swami Vivekananda

We have a master teacher inside of us and we are continually placed in situations where we have to learn to face the truth. Some people may refer to this as a spirit guide, daimon, angel, that supports you and leads you in the right direction of your life. When we find ourselves in bad working and personal relationships, we are often divinely placed in these relationships to find the learning we need. I have to qualify and say, there is nothing worse than an abusive relationship and nobody deserves to experience physical or emotional abuse.

What do we need in our life for continuous learning and growth? Wherever we find ourselves we have to be honest and ask ourselves: "How have I placed myself in this situation and what do I need to do now to learn from it and move into a better situation either within or outside the relationship?"

By not learning from our mistakes we continue to repeat the mistakes of our past. Our internal teacher must always be trusted. We forget that what we need on this earth has already been provided, we fail to see it or in our own failing, we destroy it. Don't fail to see what you have, or see it and fail to take the opportunities you are shown. Again, we must start by being honest with ourselves and trusting our inner feelings. How many times have you felt or known that something is just not right for you, but acted contrary to your feelings? We may think that it is easier to ignore the inner truth –

but somehow it will catch up with you in the end. Often avoidance takes the form of substitutes like alcohol, drugs, over or under eating.

> *"Trust your own instincts, they are usually right"*

The people we connect with and the environments we stay in, will either add or take away from our growth in this world. Coming to terms with what is right for us is difficult. Change is not easy and sometimes for a period of time can feel hurtful. Growing into who we are and who we must become may take us on paths that are uncertain and fearful. Learning to trust from within does not come easy. Learning comes from both positive and negative experiences in our life. Forgiveness, for ourselves and to others in our life is important to enable growth. It is easier to create internal stories in our minds that we were right and the other person was wrong.

These are our own stories of which we all have our own perspective. Does the truth lay with your version of a story or with someone else's? Where does the truth lay?

I have struggled at times with this journey and wasted my time with my own mind games. Not seeking to learn and grow. As fathers we see the good in our children and wish for them a happy life. Sometimes, hopefully seeking it to be happier than we feel our own life is. Yet reverse the question and all your children desire for you is happiness in your life. Be careful, there is a difference between happiness and selfishness. In business you may be presented with an opportunity that serves another's personal objectives and not your own growth.

Seeking happiness for your kids is supporting them in what they want and not what you want. As parents we sometimes pressure our kids to be who we wanted to be and therefore, seek the opportunity to live that life through them. It is important to help them find their own gifts and give them the time to come to terms with their gifts. For some people, they may not witness their gifts in this world. As a parent we must be there to gently guide and support them as necessary. Encourage them to seek the master teacher within, their child.

One of my sons is excellent at drawing and sketching. I can also say he is excellent at lots of things. He has a great capacity to see the answer to mathematical problems and the shape of a mechanical drawing in the question. In school, his teachers were very impressed. At the age of 11 he was attending classes with mathematic questions set for university level students. One day, I asked him: "how do you know the answers so easily? How are you able to do the mechanical drawings so quickly?" He responded by saying:

93

"I just see the answers to the maths questions and the shape of the drawings in my head and I just draw what I see." I think this is a great gift. His gift may not involve working in the area of mathematics or technical drawing for him, but may guide him in being honest within and trusting that he has the gift to see the answer to problems when they are set in front of him. To seek out his potential and know where he finds his happiness in his growing in both his personal and business worlds.

We must refocus our mindset to use our common sense as a child would do. A child would not follow a leader or individual whose values were self-serving and selfish. The American natives and Canadian aboriginal people have a healthy mindset when it comes to children. The elders continually and consistently watch the children play to see who the natural leaders are within their community. The elders then converse with each other and collectively decide who they will educate and guide in their ways of leadership. Starting at a very young age they will plant the seeds and instill the values of community, responsibility, and respect for each other, so that they will become the best leader they can. Their leaders do not gain leadership control through the bullying of others; which is often seen today in many organizations and leadership of countries. Watching the children play, so that the leader they choose, will demonstrate caring for the community and their environment, so that future generations will also share in what this earth can naturally provide for; our well-being. And not the leaders that will rape its natural resources, enslave and torture its people. Support war for the selfish good of a few, controlled by self-serving corporations. Individuals who have no moral questions in their vocabulary only profit.

We all have many inner gifts, finding them is our journey through life. We can hide behind false comforts to avoid facing our honest self. Trusting the inner child who is our teacher that we have been given, and those who we know as our true friends. Our soul mates are our supports that add to our growth. When it feels right, it is right. You can never be wrong when you do what is right. Reflect on the challenge of being honest with yourself and those whom enter your environment for the next 48 hours. I suggest that you read once a day for the next 90 days the words contained within *Guidance in your world* to support you. (you will find it at the back of the book).

Our inner teacher sits in our curiosity, dreams and values which in turn tries to protect us from our continuous limiting beliefs.

"Our inner teacher, our sixth sense, is our authentic self." - Angie Karan

"Life is difficult but we can make it more difficult for ourselves when we are not travelling the road we know we should."

My page for notes, scribbles, drawing or doodling

What is one thing I will do next?

My page for notes, scribbles, drawing or doodling

Chapter Eight

Dreams, Values & Self-Limited Beliefs

Alice laughed. "There's no use trying," she said: "one can't believe impossible things."

"I daresay you haven't had much practice," said the Queen. "When I was your age, I always did it for half-an-hour a day. Why, sometimes I've believed as many as six impossible things before breakfast."

As children we have faith in our direction and that one day we will grow up and be the person or super hero that we have dreamt about. It is for all of us to be the best version of ourselves that we can. Do you think for one minute that whoever created us, be that from the heavens, energies of the universe or actually the basic act of intercourse by our parents, that our creator would not want to create us to be the best

101

creation possible? Does a manufacturer of products want to invent or produce products that malfunction? The question I hear you say is: "What about those born with what we have attributed the name disability?" Children with visible disabilities are created perfectly in their world and are children from the universe who can teach us lessons about life. We all have disabilities in our lives, mostly none visible. Facing and admitting to them is our difficultly. Having grown up with my uncle Johnny, who was a child from the heavens. Johnny was labelled with what is known as Down Syndrome. I can never be more thankful for the lessons he shared with me and my family for being who he was in this world. It is important to remind ourselves that no matter what, we all have dreams.

As we grow, our dreams are changed by the control structures, institutions and

102

organizations that we are sent to learn from. Associating with individuals that don't share the same values. Audrey, my best friend in life, often recalls her first day in school. Age four years, Audrey and another girl named Helene were dancing around the classroom, each with a little chair on their head. When the teacher entered the room to meet her new class of four and five year olds, she immediately reprimanded Audrey and her friend Helene. The teacher made them stand facing into a cupboard. Thus, the beginning of the removal of the free spirit of the child and welcoming them to control and authority. I am delighted to say that Audrey took wonder in all the magical things that she could see in the class cupboard and to this day demonstrates her free spirit in the world. In the world of business on your first day in the workplace the company often replicates the removal of free spirit with their induction programme. This is the way we do things around here, so get in line.

From a very early age we are taught obedience and conformity in our school system. Our sense of free spirit of curiosity, skills of creativity, imagination, and free thinking are removed. So that, when we enter the workplace, we do so as slaves. One may go through 12 to 14 years of school training to, behave, conform and take orders of control. Organisations want us to behave in a way that suit their needs. By which we are then judged. We operate like Robots. You may have heard the saying: "I am just another cog in the machine". But we are not Robots we are people with emotions. Organisations very often say one thing and behave differently. There is nothing within the organisations that encourages individuals to grow and become who they are meant to be. Most importantly, we give up our dreams to work in the world of business rather than playing and living our values that are within. We lose our child within and conform. We let go of our dreams and abide by the values of others, be they good or bad.

> *The future belongs to those who believe in the beauty of their dreams.* - ELEANOR ROOSEVELT

Research those that dropped out of school and the structured education system early on, see how they succeeded in their world. For example, here are a very few of many: Richard Branson, Francios Pinault, David Murdock, George Foreman, Joe Lewis, Philip Emeagwali, Mangus Walker, Bill Gates and Steve Jobs. Yes, on the downside there are thousands of entrepreneurs for whom things did not quite work out. The commonality is the willingness to listen to the inner self and take the risk. With risk comes possible failure with failure comes learning. We learn more from our real-world interactions than in a classroom. Assess your risks and get on with it. It is better to say I tried, than I never even tried.

I spent most of my school days learning compulsory rubbish and having to sit through tests to regurgitate what I had learned. The rest of my days I spent on the mich (skipping school or truancy) with Joey McCann and enjoying the world by exploring what was out there. The tests did not prepare me to work with anyone or build relationships. Group learning subjects would have been better, where we have to work things out, get along with people, as in the real world. I was never asked to name any of the capital cities of the world at any job interview I attended, nor was I ever asked to discuss the works of Shakespeare or what did I think of King Lear's decisions around his daughters.

What value does our current class structure have, other than instilling conformity and removing our curiosity. The school system has not really changed much over the years and I believe it has one function, that being: Of control to enslave you to the workplace. There is division within the schooling system in both public and private schools. Having attended the right school gets played out in the workplace.

> *Parents and schools should place great emphasis on the idea that it is all right to be different. Racism and all the other 'isms' grow from primitive tribalism, the instinctive hostility against those of another tribe, race, religion, nationality, class or whatever. You are a lucky child if your parents taught you to accept diversity. - Roger Ebert*

Individuals seem to leave the structured school system with the notion that they are all going to get A's and make a difference in the world of business. It seems nowadays that if a child has an issue at school Mum or Dad will sort it out and reprimand the teacher. The parents

107

have forgotten that this does not prepare their child for the real world. There is an increase in non-denominational schools and home schooling by parents who wish to create a better learning environment for their children.

What would our junior school years have been like, had we the same freedom as at university level? Come and go as we please, participate in the subjects that we were interested in. If the school system has removed your creativity, your self beliefs and dreams of what could be, awaken yourself and seek back your inner child. Following your dreams and values in life is difficult but, very achievable if you seek that inner strength of the child. Duplicating the educational system in Finland is a great example of how schooling should be implemented.

If you are currently working- employed by an organization, ask yourself the following questions: -

- Am I having fun working here?
- What makes me get up every day to come to work for this organisation?
- What are the values of this organisation and do they match my values?
- Is this organization supporting my growth in life?
- Would I want any of my children to work here?
- Am I happy here?
- Have I lost my childhood dreams?
- Am I accepting that this is the best it will get in my life?
- If I had the option to give up my job today would I?
- What would I really do to fill my dreams?

Lots of organisations have terms like *'our people are our most important asset'*. Of course you are, until the restructure. Is there a difference between the values written down by the organisation and the demonstration of these values in your workplace? If there is a mismatch what are you doing about it? If you are the owner, Chairperson, CEO Managing Director responsible for leading the organisation and there is a mismatch, then you have an even greater responsibility to make changes. As a CEO or owner, do you even actually know if there is a mismatch? Too often I have seen weak leadership, in what people say the organisation's values are and how people behave against these communicated values. As the leader, the further away you are from the grass roots of the organization, the greater the opportunity for the gap in behaviours. Children are small and closer to the ground. Closer to the ground in business is closer to the reality of what is happening. The owners, CEOs must be like the child and become closer to the ground, with their clients, employees and suppliers.

Here are some of my suggested values. They may not be perfect but it's a start. They may not be the most well written values, but does this matter if behaviours are demonstrated through actions? The most important issue is that we are able to live by them.

OUR VALUES ARE ABOUT:

- **Openness** - Having excellent communications with each other and our clients.
- **Client First** - Having the discipline, commitment and determination to deliver for each other and our clients.

- **Learning** - Having care for our own personal growth, in our business and personal environments.

- **Integrity** - Having trust in our colleagues and building trust with our clients through honesty.

- **Fun** - Having and creating fun. Laughing every day and having fun in all that we do.

- **Encouragement** - Encouraging the child within us all to grow and live so that we feel good about what we do. Honouring our failures, for we know the journey is as important as the result.

- **Respect** - Creating a safe playground for us all to play in. Support each other to achieve our dreams as we live by respect for each other.

Could you live with these values and more importantly, could you deliver these values through your behaviours? If you desire change, then it is your people that will bring it about, so yes, the focus is on YOU. We need to dare to be different.

> *If there's any message to my work, it is ultimately that it's OK to be different, that it's good to be different, that we should question ourselves before we pass judgment on someone who looks different, behaves different, talks different, is a different color. - Johnny Depp*

Like parents of children we only wish the very best for them and to be happy in whom they want to become. It takes courage and strength in being a unique person as we all are created uniquely. Do you really think the banking system or other large corporations really care about your dreams and values? We have seen by the behaviours within the banking sector they only care about one thing, thier money and not you. How many people do the bankers talk to, if they don't have any money?

You could work with an amazing organisation where people really matter and they allow for growth. Where you can, play and have fun without fear. Remember as a child we all got to play in the games, even if you were the person to keep watch. As long as you try your hardest you will always get to play. A question you can ask yourself is - am I getting **on** in my life or getting **by**? It is not what happens to you, but what you do and how you react with what happens that shapes your future. Success and failures open up possibilities in your life. You can make that difference. Never lose you, because you are unique and you should always want that distinction. Lose those self-limited thoughts and your fears of failing. Do the work you need to deliver on your dreams. Honouring the child within requires confidence. Watch a child dance and play, they shine from within and have no regard for those who may be watching. They ask why and point out things that they don't understand. The child says how they feel and states the obvious. There is no reason for hurt in their questions - they ask **why** to gain understanding and reason.

What stops us from following our dreams? As previously said, most schooling structures are a good place to start. Where it is hard to focus beyond the belief that: "One must get a job earn money and pay taxes – we are taught - this is success". The answer to the question: Who measures our success, is ourselves and not the system? What are we worried about, is it failure or what others may think of us? Are we hiding from our own truth?

As a child I always gave and received hugs. I told my parents that I loved them (not too often) and they told me the same (not too often but I felt it). My dad was more of the hugger – I have fond memories of him acting like a child. I do realize that many of you may have had difficult childhoods and reflecting back could be painful. I feel, though, that as an adult it should not stop you from living the childhood you wished you had. Moving forward with the positive inner child within you. With my own children when they drew a picture, I would show it off to friends and then stick it on the refrigerator for all to see. Often I would bring their little piece of artistry to my office and stick it on my wall board. Something I am sure parents can relate to. Funny, how we had these pictures in our offices but, failed to acknowledge the real value of them in the workplace.

I hope my excitement and actions encouraged my kids to make more drawings. I would often give them feedback on how great they were. Again, I hope that this supported their growth in confidence. They are the best as far as I am concerned, but of course I am biased. Our parents want us to be and think we are the best – yet we don't seem to believe in their confidence of us – maybe we should have listened more? One of the most important teachings a parent can offer their children is to respect others in this world. Not to think they are better than others, especially those that have lost their way in this world. It is regretful that there are evil people who carry out evil acts and I do believe they will receive their justice in another world.

In the business world we start making comparisons with others. What is this all about? Who decides the measures of success in your life? Who or what are you comparing yourself to? What comparisons are you making in your personal and business world? I would suggest that you stop right now and ask yourself what is important to you and who is important to you right now in your life? Only you can decide the measures of success in your life.

Comparing yourself to others is pointless as you are unique and beautiful in your own way. There is no one else like you in this world, we are all made special for a reason. We often spend our time worrying about what people think of us and then realise that it really does not matter.

> *"What other people think about you is not your business. If you start to make that business your business, you will be offended for the rest of your life."-* Deepak Chopra

You set your own measures of success in this life. How you show up each day telling yourself how great you are. Love yourself and tell those that matter in your life that they are important to you and that you care for them. Be very careful how you let others influence or lead you astray. I have memories of my mum saying: *'That boy is a bad influence on you – you best stay clear of him,'* rings in my ears.

You are the designer of your own life. Don't hinder your growth by holding on to past issues and thoughts. Your journey is part of your success and is just as important as the results it produces. Getting beyond the main focus of money and a job – awakens your inner being or guide to support you in the successes only you need. So are you getting **on** or getting **by**? – revisit your dreams and values and make sure you are creating your own measure of success. If you live from that deeper place of the child within, you can ripen like a fruit.

What gets honoured in a Country gets done –Plato

What is honoured in your world?

Be curious about what you want. You may surprise yourself with what you can achieve. Do not destroy or limit your beliefs. Here is a short list of the common blockages or limiting beliefs:

- It is too risky or I'm fearful of change;
- What if it does not work?
- I don't have enough money;
- I don't have the courage;
- I am not good enough;
- I don't deserve it;
- My friends may not like me if I change.

The individuals that have achieved greatness in their lives had their own limiting beliefs, but they managed to rise above them. Children don't consider self-limiting beliefs as they have not yet been affected by the thoughts of others. As a child, we would get up to all sorts of crazy shit. When I look back I wonder where I got the courage. The thing is, no one told me I couldn't do it. Yes, children get scared sometimes, but they communicate their feelings and seek comfort in the support of their parents. In our world of business, we hold our feelings and fears inside. To share how we are feeling may be met with resistance and opposition.

Remember when getting ready to make changes in your circumstances it is okay:

- To be scared and frightened about things;

- To be confused about where you are now in your life;

- To be honest with yourself about your feelings;

- To be yourself and who you really are;

- To share how you feel with others;

- To dream;

- To have that fantasy;

- To start over again;

- To have plans;

- To do the things you need to do;

- To not have to compete with others;

- To want to be better;

- To love;

- To love yourself;

- To want to be loved;

- To apologize;

- To forgive;

- To dislike some individuals (because you don't like them does not necessarily mean they don't have other friends);

- To decide to deal with an issue later (but know you will have to deal with it and you can't avoid it);

- To say No;

- To take time for yourself;

- To hate your job;

- To love your job;

- To feel happy;

- To feel sad;

- To laugh;

- To have fun in your life;

- To keep things simple in your life;

- To be alone;

- To relax and chill.

It's not okay to do nothing about how you are feeling if it is affecting your own growth in life. It's not okay to disallow yourself to learn, grow, and be who you know you should be.

> *"It's easy to have faith in yourself and have discipline when you're a winner, when you're number one. What you've got to have is faith*

and discipline when you're not yet a winner."
Vince Lombardi

Recognise what your self-limiting beliefs are and rise above them. Sometimes it's as simple as telling yourself: "I can do it". Keep repeating this to yourself because you are now creating a belief in yourself that you can do this. Get focused, be focused and stay focused on your dreams. You will already communicate better with those you come in contact with each day. Being honest with yourself and others will provide you with a feeling of self-satisfaction.

The words like: "Stuck in this job" will start to become more unstuck, as you realise you have choices. You choose how to think and behave within a job or personal relationship. Even if it's starting to reflect and you think differently.

> *"I'm convinced that we can write and live our own scripts more than most people will acknowledge. I also know the price that must be paid. It's a real struggle to do it. It requires visualization and affirmation. It involves living a life of integrity, starting with making and keeping promises, until the whole human personality the senses, the thinking, the feeling, and the intuition are ultimately integrated and harmonized".* - Stephen Covey

It is time to try something new. Time to do what you have always wanted to do. Now is the time to make things happen for you and not to you. You may have decided to set yourself up in your own business or with a new partner. Whichever you have decided to do, make sure you represent yourself in the first instance. You have this opportunity to start out the way you want to. Do what you have always wanted to do. "What about earning money?", I hear. Believe me, do what your passion is or live with regret for the remainder of your life. Happiness comes first, bringing fun and growth into your world. The money may follow. Too many people spend their time chasing money, which they never catch. Let the money chase you. Don't ever let it hold you back from being who you need to be. Go play like a child and enjoy the fun you will bring to others.

There is a difference between seeking your dreams and wasting your time – only you will know the difference. That is why it is important to be honest with yourself. Don't get confused with giving up on your dreams and wasting time. Children dance as if nobody is watching them, so should we all. Some people spend half of their lives worrying about what other people think of them and the other half of their lives worrying that nobody really gave two flying fucks. Only the important people in your life really care about you. All they want for you is for you to be healthy, happy and to dance like nobody is watching.

In times of change, what is most important is what you think about you. This is where your energy and concentration must be spent. Delete all the negatives thoughts that you may have, (e.g. I'm too old, I'll never get a new job, I don't have the skills, etc.) Negative thinking will only give you the results you don't want: - No job or business success. You have the power to change your thoughts. If you don't like the ones you have press fast forward in your brain and get yourself a new thought. Children don't hang around, they get up and get at it for it's a new bright day in their world and an opportunity to explore, imagine, create and play. Believe in yourself and what you have to offer.

What value do you put on your knowledge, experience, skills and attitude for work? If you don't value yourself, how can you expect others to? Your new business customers or employer are looking for someone who is confident; someone that can add value to their business. They are looking for someone who can solve their issues. Remember your new clients or employer are buying you, so don't undersell yourself. You are seeking to release the child within and have fun in what you do or create. Try new things and seek opportunities, think outside the normal jobs or business opportunities you may have considered before. You never know what you can achieve until you try. Use the curiosity and imagination of your inner child and play with your ideas, get excited about what could be possible in your life. The Chinese use two brush strokes to write the word 'crisis'. One brush stroke stands for danger; the other for opportunity. In a crisis, be aware of the danger, but recognise the opportunity.

> *Determination gives you the resolve to keep going in spite of the roadblocks that lay before you.* – DENIS WAITLEY

In David McNally's book titled: "Even Eagles Need a Push: Learning to Soar in a Changing World", he gives a very good description of encouragement for making that jump in your life.

> *"The eagle gently coaxed her offspring toward the edge of the nest. Her heart quivered with conflicting emotions as she felt their resistance to her persistent nudging. 'Why does the thrill of soaring have to begin with the fear of falling?' she thought. This ageless question was still unanswered for her.*
>
> *As in tradition of the species, her nest was located high on the shelf of a sheer rock face. Below there was nothing but air to support the wings of each child. "Is it possible that this time it will not work?" she thought. Despite her fears, the eagle knew it was time, her parental mission was all but complete. There remained one final task – THE PUSH.*

129

The eagle drew courage from an innate wisdom. Until her children discovered their wings, there was no purpose for their lives outside the nest. Until they learned to soar, they would fail to understand the privilege it was to have been born an eagle. The push was the greatest gift she had to offer. It was her supreme act of love. And so, one by one, she pushed them and they flew".

In this analogy I must be both the Mother and baby eagles, I must have the courage to create the changes. I must resist my inner fears and believe that the adventures of finding out who I am begins with my fears of failure. With my childlike curiosity and my imagination and adventure I must learn to soar.

"Dreaming is one of humanity's greatest gifts. It champions aspiration, spurs innovation, leads to change and propels us forward. In a world without dreams, there would be no adventure, no moon landing, no female CEOs, no civil rights. What a half-lived and tragic existence we would have. We should all dream big, and encourage others to do so, too." – Richard Branson

130

"We don't stop playing because we grow old;
We grow old because we stop playing"-
George Bernard Shaw

My page for notes, scribbles, drawing or doodling

What is one thing I will do next?

My page for notes, scribbles, drawing or doodling

"We nurture our creativity when we release our inner child.

Let it run and roam free. It will take you on a brighter journey." - Serina Hartwell

Chapter Nine

Time for Meetings or Playing

The only thing we all have that is equal is, TIME. We all have sixty minutes in one hour. Whether you are rich poor, male, female, president of a country or living on the streets. Whatever ethnic or religious group that you may or may not be associated with, you only have sixty minutes in an hour. How, with whom, and what you spend your time on is important. You can decide to spend it wisely or waste it. Remember you can lend a friend or colleague €20 euro and they can always pay it back at some stage. If somebody asks you to spend time with them, say 20 minutes, you will never get this time back. In our business world so much of our time is wasted by others. Don't let YOURSELF or let others waste YOUR time. Time wasting is anything that distracts you from your dreams and journey in life. So stop and ask yourself, is what I am doing right now helping me to live my passion? Find the right balance as to where you spend your time and energy. Balance does not always mean 50/50. The right balance of time and energy should be spent with those that matter and on the things that are valuable to you in your world.

Business meetings should start on time and finish on time – with no exceptions. How many times has YOUR time been wasted by other people in meetings? Have you ever felt that a meeting was boring and you wanted out of there? That you would rather have some fun. To this day, I have attended very few meetings in my entire career that I would consider were exceptional meetings. Well communicated, well organised, a clear objective, decisions reached, started and finished on time. A lot of bullshit goes on in organisations, with who is invited and who is not invited to a meeting. Some people would not know if they were important enough if they did not attend meetings. Have you ever wondered why some of the attendees were at a meeting and what contribution they made? Have you ever been sent to a meeting by your manager without any clear guidance on what your role is in the meeting? The question is why are you attending and to do what? Your inner child is screaming to get out and shout out: "This is a waste of my time!".

'Say it in Six' written in the 1996 by Ron Hoff is well worth a read. Ron, talks about effective meetings. He stresses you should be able to make your pitch or presentation in six minutes or less. Ron identifies five great topic headings to support achieving a result within the time limit. They are: -

1. What is the burning issue?

2. Quick overview or background?

3. The Idea/ Solution

4. What is the Pay off?

5. What do you need from the attendees?

Using his topic headings, I would suggest that you allocate between 10 – 30 minutes only to all decision-making meetings. If the presenter(s) have identified the burning issue, some brief background that got you there, their ideas and solutions, the payoffs and what they need from the attendees at the meeting. Deliver the presentation within six minutes which will then give you 24 minutes for engagement to sign off the decision required. If you need to have another meeting after that with a different outcome and attendees then do so. Don't have individuals sitting through an hour-long meeting that could have taken 10 – 30 minutes max. Maybe there is no need to have a meeting at all;

and instead you could send out a paper with the above headings outlined. Think of the time you can now spend more productively having FUN at work. If you need a curiosity and creativity meeting, then have a longer meeting to gather thoughts and ideas only. Introduce as much fun as possible and play like children. Then follow up with your shorter 30-minute decision making meeting. We know setting a precise meeting duration helps to arrange meetings or events and gets us focused and organised. Setting a strict time limit on an activity is useful. You will see a big difference when you implement this style of meeting process. What gets focused on gets done.

We had a saying in the retail business: "Retail is detail". When you know where your time is being wasted, you can adjust your schedule accordingly and spend more time on what is important in your life. Remember, children don't waste time, they are always active and present in their world. The most important thing you can spend time on is your own growth and development, becoming who you were meant to be.

I strongly believe that over time; as we have progressed, we have forgotten to keep the right values in our culture. Everyone seems to be in the "right now" mentality; we must be at the beck and call of our technology gadgets. There is the expectation that we must respond to every email, text, and call immediately. So ban all phones from meetings so that each attendee can listen and focus on the objectives and outcomes of the meeting. How many times do you give somebody your 100% attention? How many times do you give yourself permission to focus 100% on yourself? Ignore the excuses: "I need my phone or laptop to take notes". If this is the case, your response should be: "If you need your

140

phone or laptop to take notes, I will respect that; but that is all it should be used for during my meeting." If the individual(s) uses it to check emails, their Facebook or other social media sites then they are disrespecting you and others present at your meeting. Remember it is your meeting, how you set the culture reflects back on you.

Where and how do you want to spend your time? Deepak Chopra has spoken about "mindful living".

> *Mindful living is just the ability and responsibility to choose what and how you experience life in this very moment because all you have is the external now - all the rest is imagination.*

Often spending time with family or friends gets pushed aside as we are too busy with our own concerns around our work. I feel we have forgotten the value of time and we are not taking the time to spend time with those that are important to us and to learn and grow. We seem to have no time in our day to sit in silence and search for who we are or who we must become.

I used to work over 60+ hours a week for a large supermarket business in Ireland. 60-70 hours per week was seen as the norm in the industry. If you left the office before 6pm you would hear: "On a half day then". When I set up my own companies the hours never reduced as work was now on my mind fulltime. For most individuals, their working life is somewhere between the ages of 18/20 years old and 60/65 years old. Our very best and youthful years. You have heard me say this previously, if you are in this position and you dislike what you are doing, make the changes you need to make now. If you don't do it now, do you feel it will get any easier later on in your life? We all have so many excuses, "I have to stay in this position

142

because....", "We need the money......", "I can't change now" or "I will when .....,". You, and only you, own the decision to stay in that crap job or relationship.

I can't say that I got it right all the time with the changes I made in my life; I didn't, but I made the changes I thought were best and I took control of my life. You can't guarantee your future and how things might work out for you, but it is better you are in control of it rather than someone else. Yes, it takes courage to make a change in your life, but courage is better than regret. I decided to leave a secure job where I held a directorship. I was paid extremely well, but was unhappy with the deceit of the new cultural environment. For me, in the later 3 years I worked in a very toxic environment. Some very senior individuals stated that they held one value, yet behaved to the contrary. Leaving was one of the best decisions I ever made, it showed me more of myself and gave me the opportunity to learn and grow from within. It reminded me of some of the lessons that I had forgotten. Lessons like, honesty, being true to yourself, humility. It helped me focus through my personal learning back to the innocense of a child.

One Christmas I learned a very important lesson from my eldest son who was five years old. The supermarkets business: Anyone who has worked in this sector knows about the early mornings, late evenings and the very long hours. Often I would get up at 5:00am to travel to meeting locations across the country. Christmas time is especially a very busy and exciting period. One is often working well after the close of business on Christmas Eve. This particular Christmas Eve I finished late. When I got home I had something to eat. Organised the Santa presents out from all those hidden places and placed each present underneath the carefully decorated Christmas tree. I then sat down and had a glass of beer, and admired each of the decorations, most of which had a little story about them. I gazed at all the well-wrapped presents that would bring much joy to everyone as they ripped off the wrapping paper with excitement on Christmas morning. By this time it was now close to 1:00am, I headed off to bed. At about 5:30am my son came into our bedroom saying: "Daddy Daddy Santa has come, Santa has come." To which, I replied in a very tired voice, "it's only 5:30am and it's too early to get up for Santa. We will get up in an hour or so", trying to coax him back to bed. Without hesitation he replied, "but Daddy if you can get up for work at this time, surely you can get up for Santa." I was out of my bed so quick and down the stairs before he could catch his breath. You can see I have never forgotten this important lesson.

You can take the control over your time no matter where you are. Let the child within live and grow. We get back what we invest our time in. Start from this moment and say a special hello to a friend you may have forgotten in your life, as your time became too busy and you forgot how to play like a child. Remember those that are important to you and go play. No better time like the present.

"Your time is limited, so don't waste it living someone else's life. Don't be trapped by dogma - which is living with the results of other people's thinking. Don't let the noise of other's opinions drown out your own inner voice and most important, have the courage to follow your heart and intuition. They somehow already know what you truly want to become. Everything else is secondary. "- Steve Jobs

My page for notes, scribbles, drawing or doodling

What is one thing I will do next?

My page for notes, scribbles, drawing or doodling

Chapter Ten

Change is Not the Boogeyman

"Whoever can see through all fear will always be safe. "-Tao Te Ching

Why is it that we find change so difficult when we are continually changing? It begins with fear. How many people do you know are disruptive to change within organisations or within their lives? People seldom complain for the reasons that you think and therefore, they may be reluctant to identify that their fears are to change. Change is happening all around us, every minute of every day. We are changing ourselves so that we can grow. If we did not accept the changes in our bodies, we would die. What we fight against most is change itself. Why are so many people fearful of change in their workplace and personal lives? As children we cannot wait to grow up, sometimes too quickly. We acknowledge each day as a new adventure in our lives. What is changing is the curiosity of the child. Things that remain the same are boring. There is always our "me factor" trying to anticipate how will this change impact me? What will others think of me if I change? Are we letting change happen **to us** or letting it happen **for us** in our lives?

For example, if there are new ways of working or technologies in your workplace and you have not learned to cope with these changes, you may not survive in that environment. Using the curiosity and excitement of your child within, can make the change happen for you. You can decide to learn new ways or let change happen to you, which in turn could contribute to being ineffective in your workplace. It is not an excuse to say I am too old to change. You can always change your attitude.

Do you know what is stopping you from making these changes in your life? What are you fighting against? The most common answer, as I mentioned earlier, is fear. Alternatively, individuals state that they are very happy with the status quo and don't see the need for any change. Yet they may not acknowledge it, but changes are happening all around them and increasing their fears. Common answers come from information we have all picked up as we have grown or experienced through our lives; listening to negative thoughts from within or by others whom we surround ourselves with. As said before if you don't like a thought press forward to the next thought in your brain.

> *If you know the enemy and know yourself you*
> *need not fear the results of a hundred battles.*
> *– Sun Tzu*

Recognise your fears and learn from them, without fears you may not learn. Remember the child within you, how many times did that child stand up and try to walk, and how many times did it fall down? It continued to get up and walk until it learned how. We have forgotten our learning path of a child. Consider other successes and achievements that supported you in your growth. So what is stopping you now? Once you understand the blockages, then you can start to break down these barriers and start making the changes necessary to help you achieve what you want for your success going forward into the future. There is no better time than the present time. There is no future in the past.

You don't know what the future holds but you can surely influence it by your attitude and behaviour. How you behave and communicate; who you are is vital. How open you are to learning and watching your surrounding environment will support you in ensuring that your learning is equal to or greater than the changes happening around you. Are you present in the moment, like a child playing?

> *"If you can't explain it simply, you don't understand it well enough". - Albert Einstein*

Some of you may be feeling that it is not as easy as this. Let me tell you, it is. Where I had failed in my past is that I gave the power of control to others. I thought, if I make this change now how will it affect others. I used this as an excuse not to change. It was the courage of the child. I needed to call it as it was and not fear sharing how I felt. I spent my time thinking of others and not accepting that if I was happy so would they be.

When I decided to leave the secure job in mid-1999 and start my own business it was my decision and I took control. In the beginning I was unsure of what I would do. When you are part of a large organisation you are somewhat protected. I left not knowing my real value; I was disillusioned about culture and the falseness of certain individuals that I had supported and trusted. I had to be true to myself. I must acknowledge those whom really supported me in my decision and whose counsel I sought at the time. They know who they are.

My proudest moments quickly followed in those early days as I realised the value of my own skills and my ability to make a good living from these skills. Taking personal control of where I was at in my working and personal life picking my personal inner fights to make the changes I needed to.

I do wish I had made some changes earlier for lots of reasons and I do know that there is no point in thinking: "Only if". We are all human and no matter who you are, we do sometimes think: "Only if". I did make decisions, when the pain was too much to continue in the environment that I was in. The difference between some people is that some of us move on and don't stay in this position and others stay there and never move on. They can never leave that space they were in and they seem to never grow or find out who they can be. They are more comfortable with being the victim. This gives them their identity and a supporting mechanism to cope.

> *Without change there is no innovation, creativity, or incentive for improvement. Those who initiate change will have a better opportunity to manage the change that is inevitable. -* WILLIAM POLLARD

Recognizing that change is necessary is a good place to start. For me change was about five action steps: -

1. Starting with making small changes;

2. Identifying the blockages to change;

3. Making the commitment;

4. Focusing on the vision of what success/ achievement looks and feels like;

5. Taking the first step by breaking through my fears – and celebrating the success.

The phrase by Albert Einstein, *"if you always do what you have always done you will always get what you have always got"* comes to mind. If you are not the best you can be, then you cannot be the best for others in your life. Seth Godin does an exercise with the audience when he asks them to raise their hand as high as they can and then asks; now raise it a little higher. We all hold back a little. How do you expect to encourage, support and be there for others if you cannot be there for yourself? Don't hold back.

> *When I am working on a problem I never think about beauty. I only think about how to solve*

156

> *the problem. But when I have finished, if the solution is not beautiful, I know it is wrong. – R Buckminister Fuller*

Find the beauty in your solutions and bring that fear right out there so you can learn to conquer it. Don't wait and let it continue to conquer you. Remember that you are not alone no matter who you are, we all have our fears. What would you do if someone came to you for help and support? Would you turn them away? Would you be delighted if they asked for your help? There is someone waiting for you to ask for support. I asked for help and it was not easy. I had my stupid pride/ego, but once I asked all the support and help was there for me to accept. Often the fears we have built up inside of us do not exist in reality. I often feel that my work is not good enough and should never see the light of day. Yet I feel the encouragement from within.

Does this remind you of the conversations in the mirror: "If this happens I will do this …", I think you know what I am saying. Change is not the boogeyman in your life.

Our doubts are traitors, and make us lose the good we oft might win, by fearing to attempt. - William Shakespeare

"Life isn't about finding yourself. Life is about creating yourself. - George Bernard Shaw

"Celebrate your life, you are your own light"
– Lailah Gifty Akita

Chapter Eleven

Reminding Thoughts

Seek and find your direction in life through your inner child. Play like that child within and bring it forward in your life. Choose to be that happy child. Remember, if you don't know where you are going how do you expect to get there?

Following your direction means growing. Growing, happens when we take personal responsibility for the changes we want to make in our world; change is in your hands. The business world will act to discourage you from bringing and expressing childlike qualities in the workplace. I would encourage you to be brave. It is okay to be scared, but don't be afraid of doing. Our savvy child within us wants to be able to play together, share together, laugh together and look out for each other even in difficult times.

Fun & laughter must never be lost in our business world, for it is when we are having fun that we know we are alive. I would encourage you to make someone smile every day and bring laughter back into the work place. We have seen and experienced the dishonesty and lack of transparency in our governments, banks and other worldwide institutions. You can only start with your attitude and control the changes that will come to your life. The best start is to be honest with yourself and ask the questions a child would ask to both yourself and others. Out of the mouth of the child comes wisdom of seeking truth and telling it as it is, *"the Emperor has no cloths ..."*

A good starting place, that is more childlike would be to communicate with your feelings and emotions. We are emotional beings not robots. We have feelings, desires and fears. The business world is only beginning to come to terms with accepting and valuing the expressions of one's emotions. Don't leave your emotions outside the meeting room; communicate how you feel. Of course one wants to feel safe to be able to express their feelings. By sharing our feelings; we make ourselves vulnerable to others. People often say that they seek intimacy in their relationships, intimacy involves opening up and being vulnerable. In organisations it starts with the culture. If the top management are rotten and allow bullying and harassment to exist, well you best consider your options. As indicated previously, it all begins with the CEO, as it is said *"the fish smells from the head"*. Create that safe playground in your world where respect for others strives.

The people we connect with and the environments we stay in, will either add or take away from our growth in this world. Change is not easy and sometimes, for a period of time, can feel hurtful. Asking our inner teacher and listening to our gut feelings is vital. Learning to trust from within does not come easy. Learning comes from both the positive and negative experiences in our lives. Forgiveness, for ourselves and to others in our lives is important to enable growth. Seek your inner teacher to guide you in your world and practice by sitting quietly for 10- 15 minutes per day and asking yourself the questions you need answers too. The more consistently you practice this exercise the more clarity you will receive.

Are you getting by in life or are you **getting on**, the question is only for you to answer. Getting on will support you in achieving your dreams and living by your values. Self-limiting beliefs will hold you in the place of **getting by.** Dream like that child within and seek your passion. Be kind to yourself and don't measure your success by what others do or may think of you. Everyone else is trying to find out who they are and are busy with their own lives. Being who you are meant to be is all the success you need. Seek the answer in your own honesty. Even eagles need a push.

We have all heard sayings like: "life is short" or "life is short eat the dessert first". Ask that inner child, who and what is important in your life. We all have sixty minutes in one hour, what are you doing with your time. Is it time for meetings or playing in your life?

Change is not the boogeyman in your life. Change is growth, allow your inner child out to guide your way. Play and laugh like that child you used to know and bring it to all your world.

165

Reminding Thoughts

Dance Your Way to the New

Dance, dance in the wind of life

Glad you were here and now going to your new
beginning

For your work is almost done

You were once the new, busting with foliage,
busting out,

Laughing for the world with joy, shouting out,
"I am here, look at me"

Your frame and structure to support you high
and standing tall,

Look up at me for this is my tree

Clothing it during the hot summer to bear fruit
and providing shelter to the animals who vacant
there

Dance, dance in the wind of life

Now show to all the other trees, you are
changing colours and the forest will show to the
sky

Your wild beauty that you show in this world,
leaving to let in the new

Nourishing the earth during the winter so your
roots do not get cold

Dance, dance in the wind of life

As you fall, standing naked for the world to see

Knowing as you came to this world with the
hope of love and you leave with the hope of
being loved

Now with your beautiful movements so elegant,
you dance in the wind of life

Will I show such beauty as I dance my way to
the new?

Mel Clifford

Guidance in Your World

When I am unsure of what I must do, send my teachers and mentors to place the lessons before me so that I can learn, understand and grow in this world. Encourage me to stay in the moment and reflect on what I must do next. Guide me in goodness only and circle my life in the light of the heavenly stars. Guide me so that I take from this earth only what I need. While I am here, my purpose is to do good and deliver to this world something special. Let me not forget my curiosity and laughter as a child.

Let me not worry about my next life for it is the lessons of this life I must learn. Before I go let me teach others the knowledge that I gain so that they can understand and receive guidance to the next.

If I fail, let me learn under your guidance to keep trying until I succeed.

Mel Clifford

169

"We are made wise not by the recollection of our past, but by the responsibility for our future"

George Bernard Shaw

Thank you for spending your time with me in reading my book and I hope that you gained something special in your world from what you have read.

Please share or gift this book with someone you feel would benefit. Change is in your hands.

Please visit my website www.melclifford.com and download and share my other EBooks

"Let us not get to the end of our life with regrets and lose that inner child, for it is through the support of your child that we will live our dreams and take the risks that will take us on our unique and special journey in this world"

Thank You

To those that took time out of their day to read a draft version of my manuscript and provide me with great suggestions and feedback.

Mr. Mark Bradley

Ms. Mary Crayn

Dr. David R. Huck, PhD, [Org. Psych], M.A., C.E.C.

Mr. Trent Jancish

Professor Suzi Jarvis

Ms. Connie Johnson

Ms. Roberta Sawatzky MA, CPHR

References

Carswell Simon, Anglo Republic: Inside the Bank that broke Ireland

https://www.penguin.co.uk/books/181757/anglo-republic/

Hoff Ron, Say it in Six

Gelb, Michael J How to think like Leonardo da Vinci Delta Trade Paperback reissue edition/ June 2004.

Miller, Michael Dr. (2005) University of Maryland Medical Center Fry, William Dr Stanford University - School of Medicine Study Shows Laughter Helps Blood Vessels Function Better – Retrieved 2015 from http://umm.edu/news-and-events/news-releases/2005/school-of-medicine-study-shows-laughter-helps-blood-vessels-function-better.

Mayo Clinic Staff April 21st 2016 Stress relief from laughter? It's no joke – Retrieved 2016 http://www.mayoclinic.org/healthy-lifestyle/stress-management/in-depth/stress-relief/art-20044456?pg=1

Morality in Islam, May 2009. Retrieved 2016 http://www.islamweb.net/en/article/134385/morality-in-islam

McNally's, David, Even Eagles Need a Push: Learning to Soar in a Changing World.

http://www.alice-in wonderland.net/resources/analysis/character-descriptions/cheshire-cat/

Clifford, Mel (2011) - Poetry Just for You

Clifford, Mel MBA, PMP, Life experiences from within and outside – www.melclifford.com

Mel has published other books and has a file of unfinished manuscripts, which he hopes to publish and share with you in the coming years.

Please visit Amazon Kindle and www.melclifford.com and download Mel's other eBooks or order printed copies.

Poetry
Just for You

Mel Clifford

Changing
the way
I am

Mel Clifford

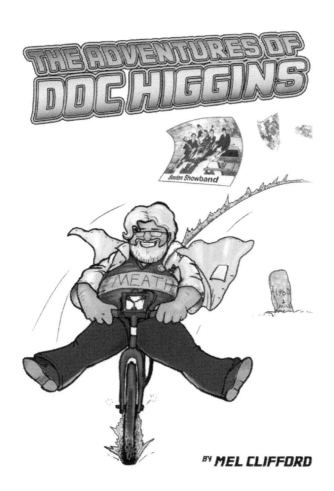

THE ADVENTURES OF DOC HIGGINS

BY MEL CLIFFORD

The Adventures of
Doc Higgins

The True Story of
King Henry VIII

Mel Clifford

The Adventures of Doc Higgins: The True Story of King Henry VIII   - Mel Clifford -

INTO
ME
I
SEE

Mel | Emily
Clifford | Elzbeth

"Life has no meaning. Each of us has meaning and we bring it to life. It is a waste to be asking the question when you are the answer." - **Joseph Campbell**

76682330R00124

Made in the USA
Columbia, SC
12 September 2017